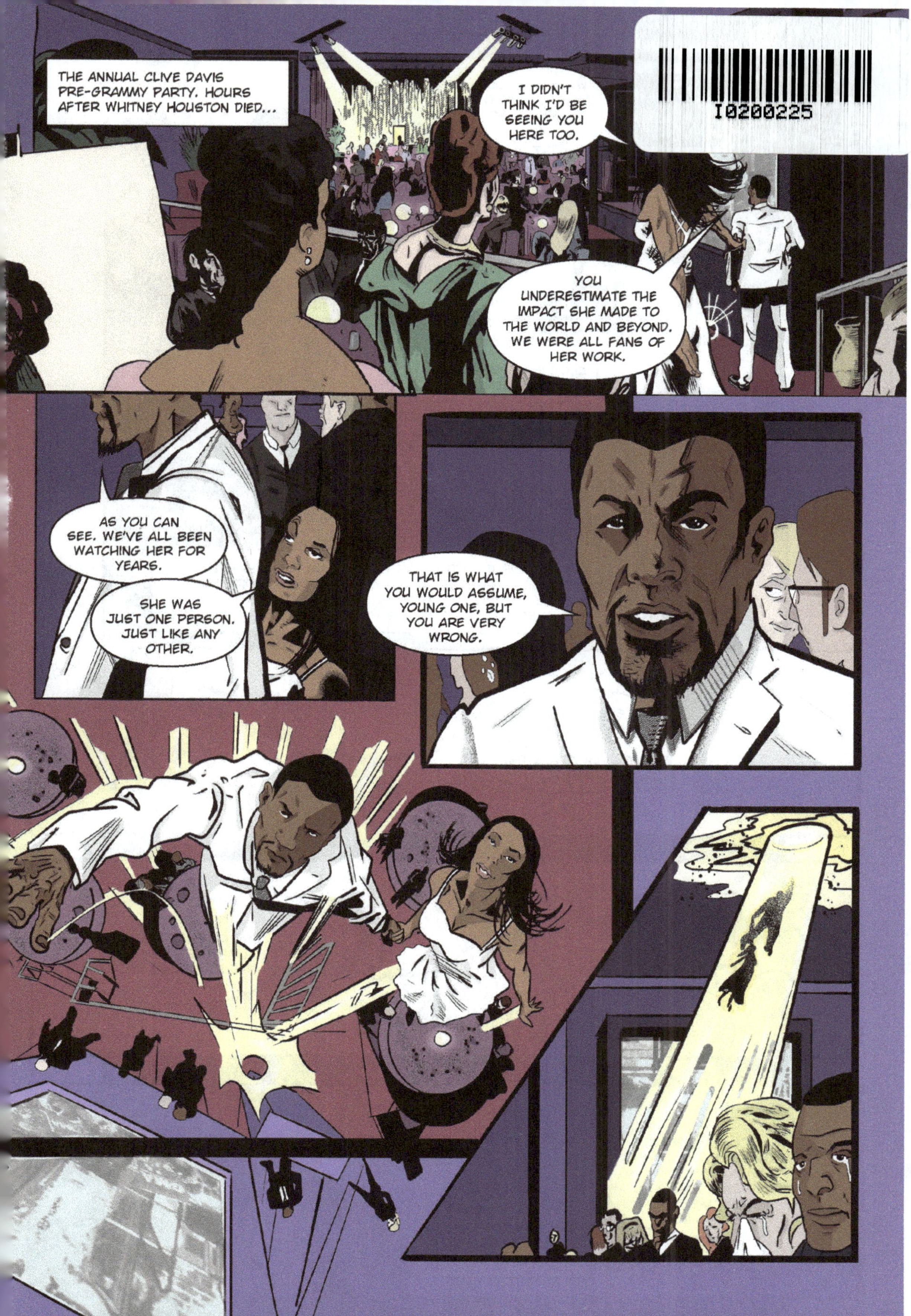
THE ANNUAL CLIVE DAVIS PRE-GRAMMY PARTY. HOURS AFTER WHITNEY HOUSTON DIED...
I DIDN'T THINK I'D BE SEEING YOU HERE TOO.
YOU UNDERESTIMATE THE IMPACT SHE MADE TO THE WORLD AND BEYOND. WE WERE ALL FANS OF HER WORK.
AS YOU CAN SEE. WE'VE ALL BEEN WATCHING HER FOR YEARS.
SHE WAS JUST ONE PERSON. JUST LIKE ANY OTHER.
THAT IS WHAT YOU WOULD ASSUME, YOUNG ONE, BUT YOU ARE VERY WRONG.

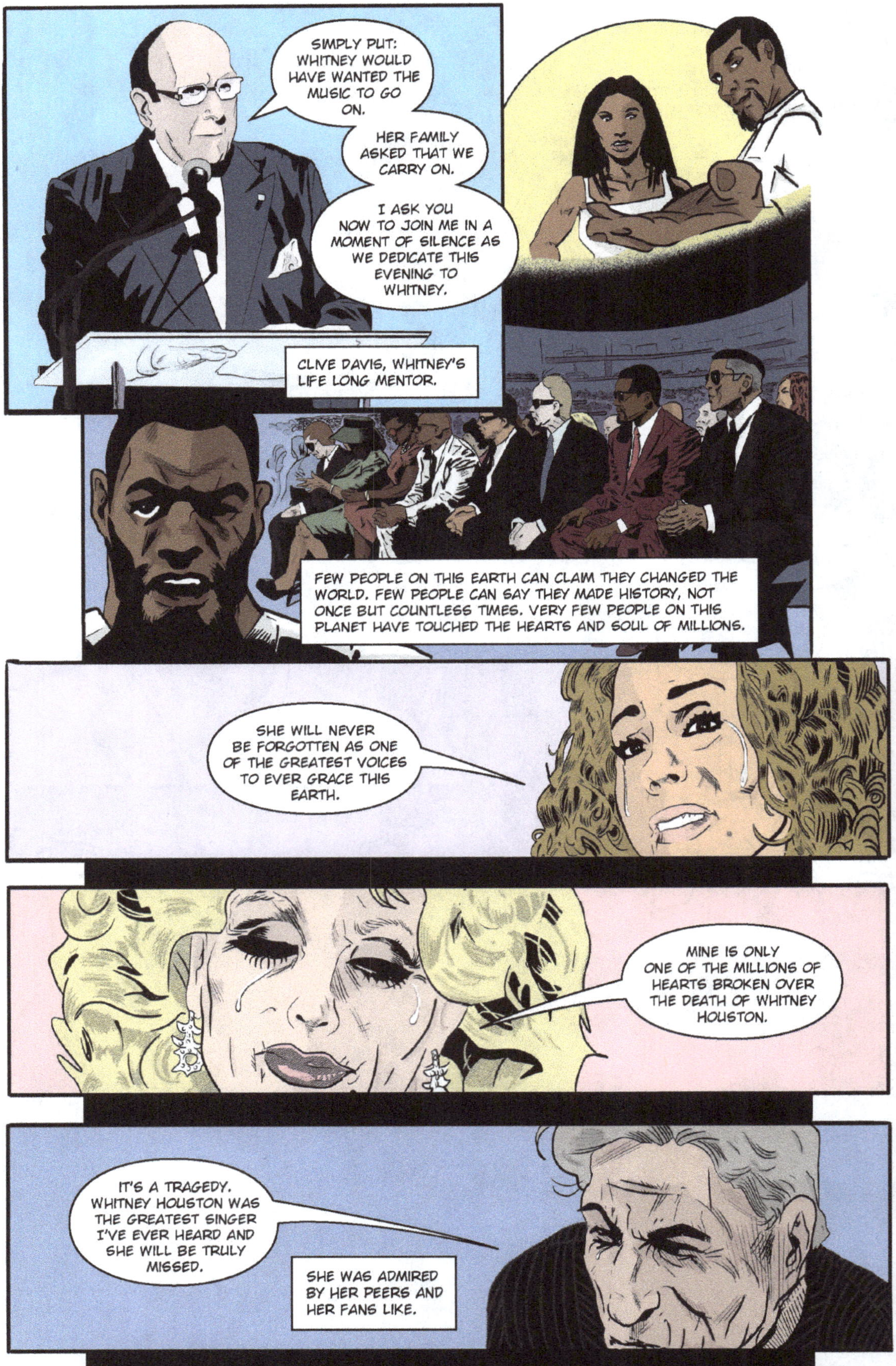
SIMPLY PUT: WHITNEY WOULD HAVE WANTED THE MUSIC TO GO ON.
HER FAMILY ASKED THAT WE CARRY ON.
I ASK YOU NOW TO JOIN ME IN A MOMENT OF SILENCE AS WE DEDICATE THIS EVENING TO WHITNEY.
CLIVE DAVIS, WHITNEY'S LIFE LONG MENTOR.
FEW PEOPLE ON THIS EARTH CAN CLAIM THEY CHANGED THE WORLD. FEW PEOPLE CAN SAY THEY MADE HISTORY, NOT ONCE BUT COUNTLESS TIMES. VERY FEW PEOPLE ON THIS PLANET HAVE TOUCHED THE HEARTS AND SOUL OF MILLIONS.
SHE WILL NEVER BE FORGOTTEN AS ONE OF THE GREATEST VOICES TO EVER GRACE THIS EARTH.
MINE IS ONLY ONE OF THE MILLIONS OF HEARTS BROKEN OVER THE DEATH OF WHITNEY HOUSTON.
IT'S A TRAGEDY. WHITNEY HOUSTON WAS THE GREATEST SINGER I'VE EVER HEARD AND SHE WILL BE TRULY MISSED.
SHE WAS ADMIRED BY HER PEERS AND HER FANS LIKE.

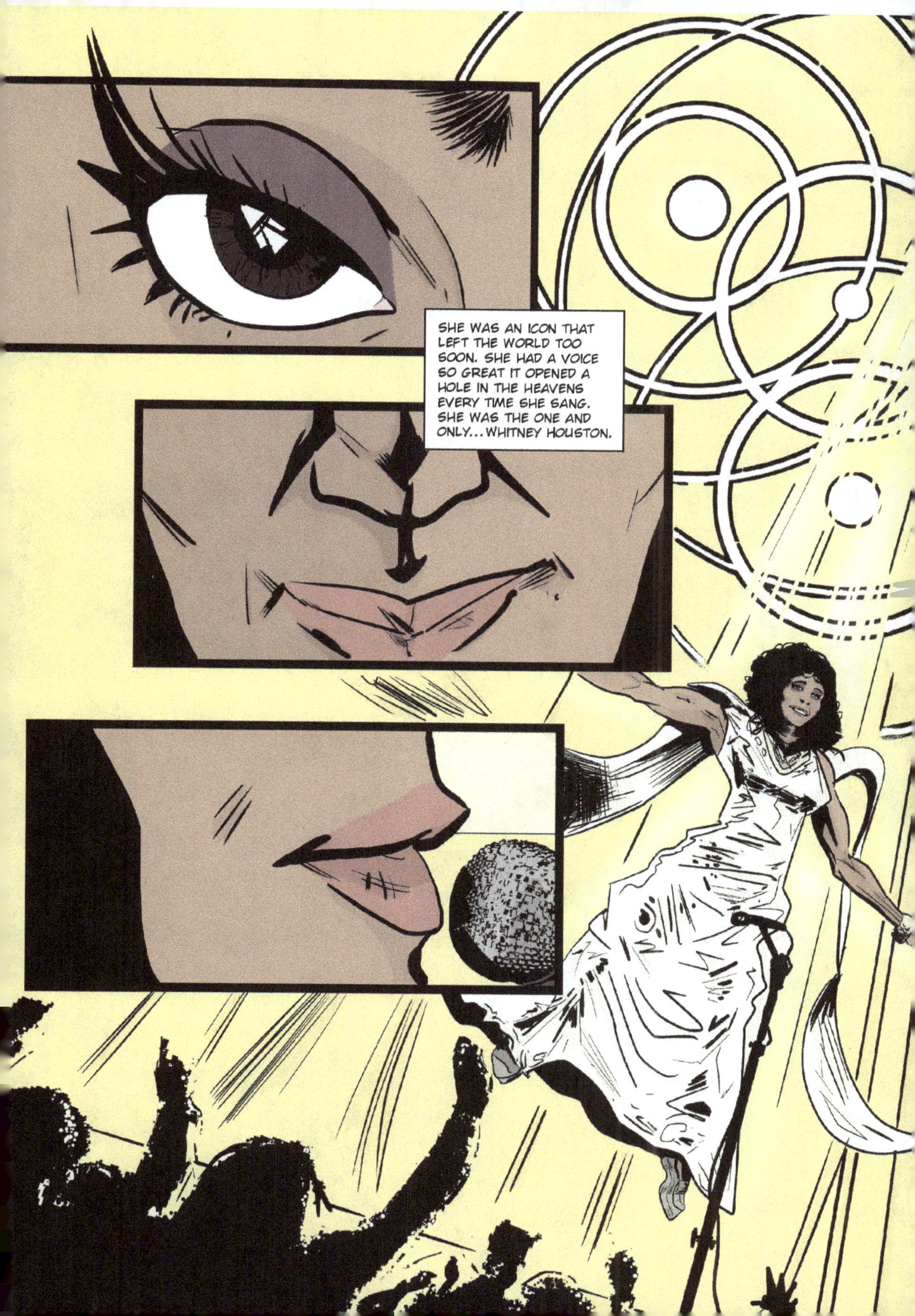
SHE WAS AN ICON THAT LEFT THE WORLD TOO SOON. SHE HAD A VOICE SO GREAT IT OPENED A HOLE IN THE HEAVENS EVERY TIME SHE SANG. SHE WAS THE ONE AND ONLY... WHITNEY HOUSTON.

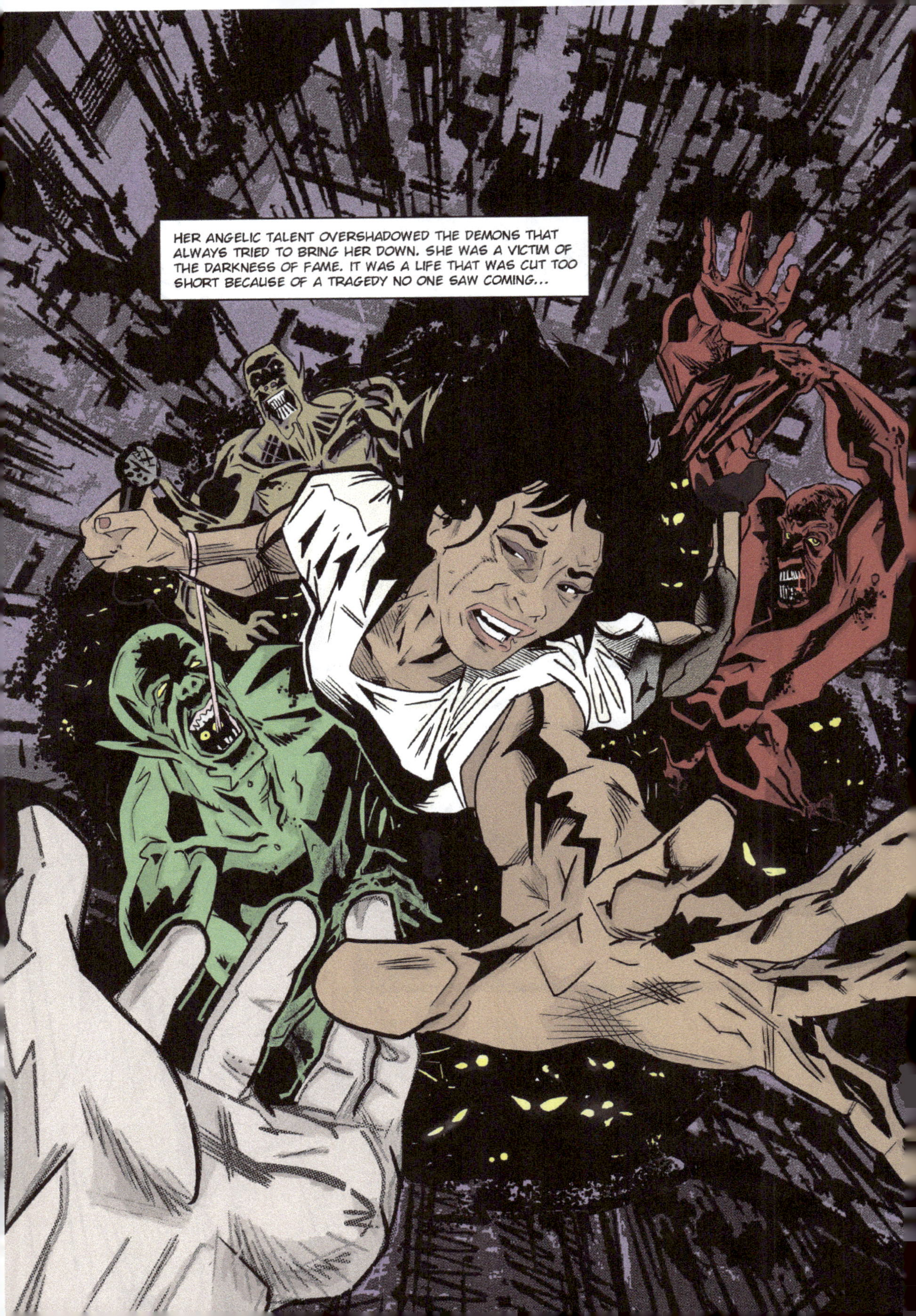
HER ANGELIC TALENT OVERSHADOWED THE DEMONS THAT ALWAYS TRIED TO BRING HER DOWN. SHE WAS A VICTIM OF THE DARKNESS OF FAME. IT WAS A LIFE THAT WAS CUT TOO SHORT BECAUSE OF A TRAGEDY NO ONE SAW COMING...

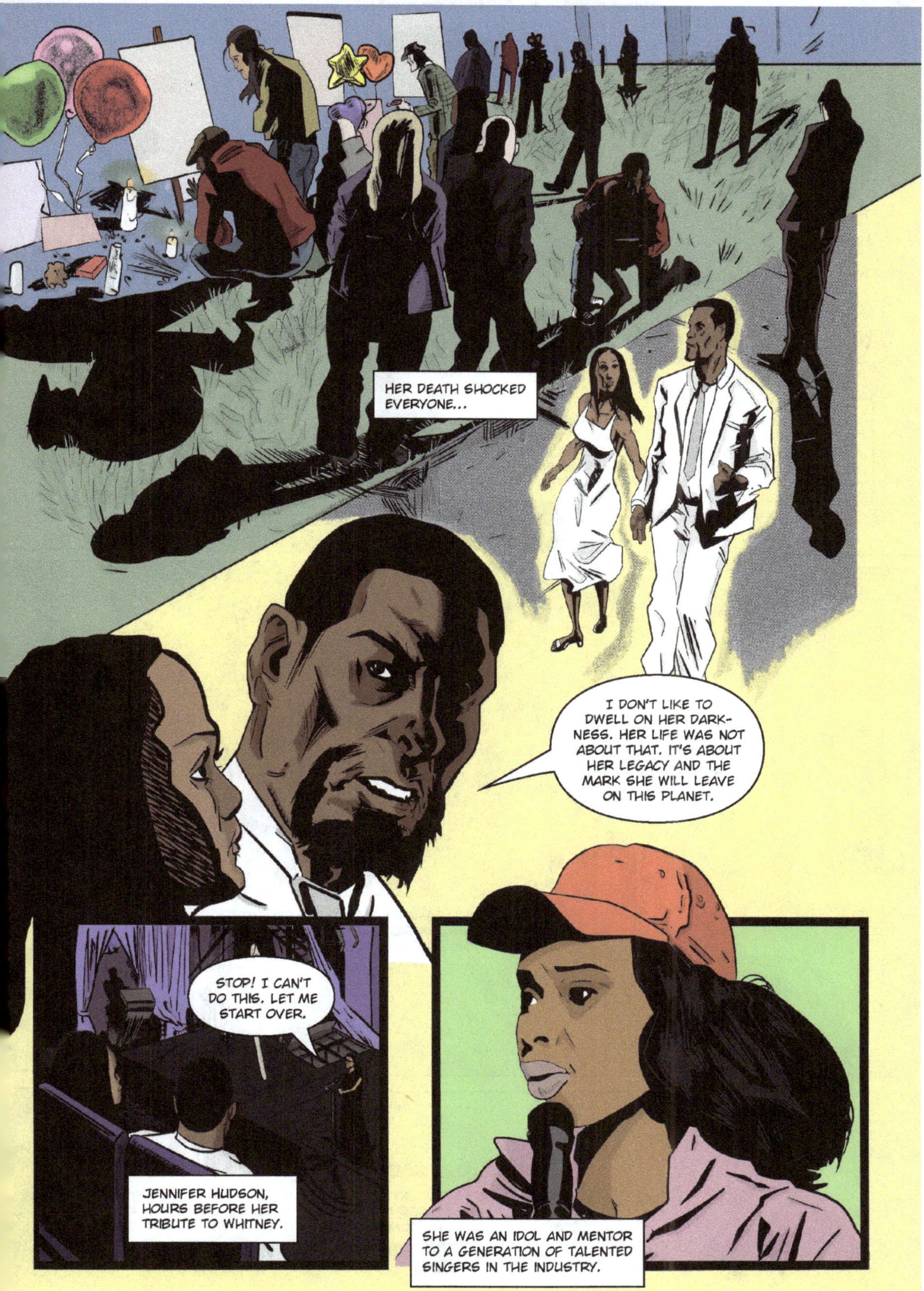
HER DEATH SHOCKED EVERYONE...
I DON'T LIKE TO DWELL ON HER DARK-NESS. HER LIFE WAS NOT ABOUT THAT. IT'S ABOUT HER LEGACY AND THE MARK SHE WILL LEAVE ON THIS PLANET.
STOP! I CAN'T DO THIS. LET ME START OVER.
JENNIFER HUDSON, HOURS BEFORE HER TRIBUTE TO WHITNEY.
SHE WAS AN IDOL AND MENTOR TO A GENERATION OF TALENTED SINGERS IN THE INDUSTRY.

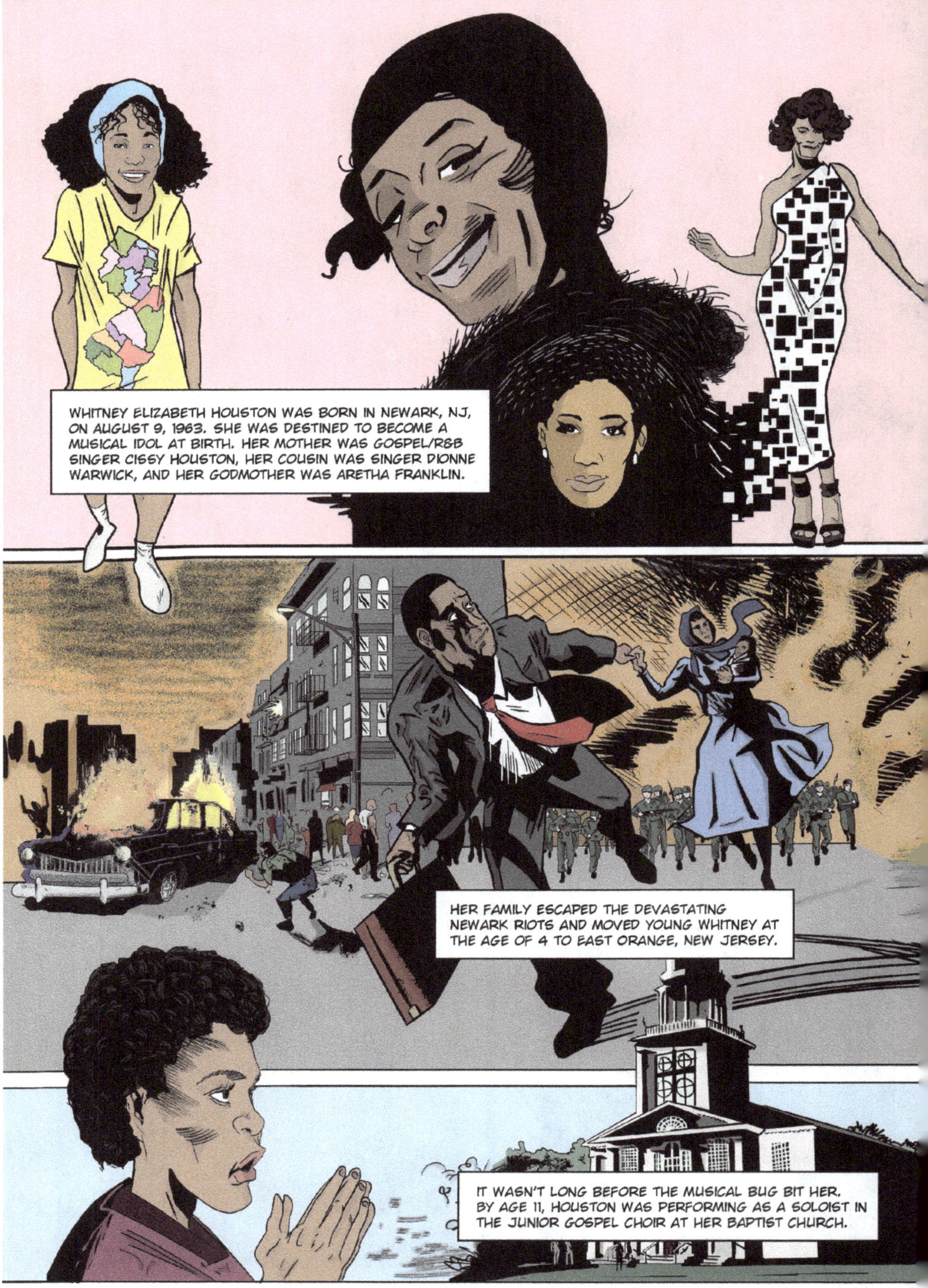
WHITNEY ELIZABETH HOUSTON WAS BORN IN NEWARK, NJ, ON AUGUST 9, 1963. SHE WAS DESTINED TO BECOME A MUSICAL IDOL AT BIRTH. HER MOTHER WAS GOSPEL/R&B SINGER CISSY HOUSTON, HER COUSIN WAS SINGER DIONNE WARWICK, AND HER GODMOTHER WAS ARETHA FRANKLIN.
HER FAMILY ESCAPED THE DEVASTATING NEWARK RIOTS AND MOVED YOUNG WHITNEY AT THE AGE OF 4 TO EAST ORANGE, NEW JERSEY.
IT WASN'T LONG BEFORE THE MUSICAL BUG BIT HER. BY AGE 11, HOUSTON WAS PERFORMING AS A SOLOIST IN THE JUNIOR GOSPEL CHOIR AT HER BAPTIST CHURCH.

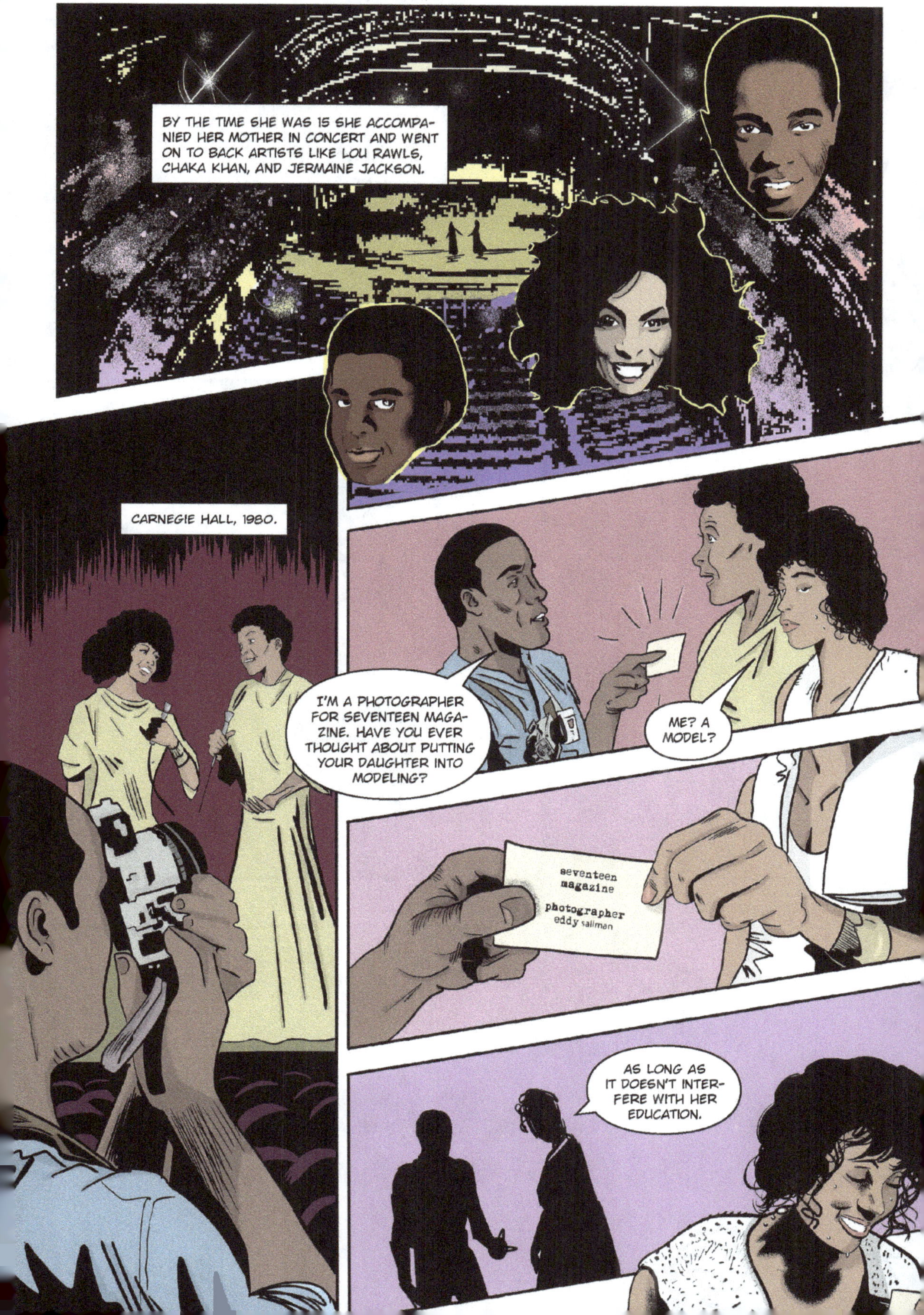
BY THE TIME SHE WAS 15 SHE ACCOMPANIED HER MOTHER IN CONCERT AND WENT ON TO BACK ARTISTS LIKE LOU RAWLS, CHAKA KHAN, AND JERMAINE JACKSON.
CARNEGIE HALL, 1980.
I'M A PHOTOGRAPHER FOR SEVENTEEN MAGAZINE. HAVE YOU EVER THOUGHT ABOUT PUTTING YOUR DAUGHTER INTO MODELING?
ME? A MODEL?
seventeen magazine
photographer
eddy sallman
AS LONG AS IT DOESN'T INTERFERE WITH HER EDUCATION.

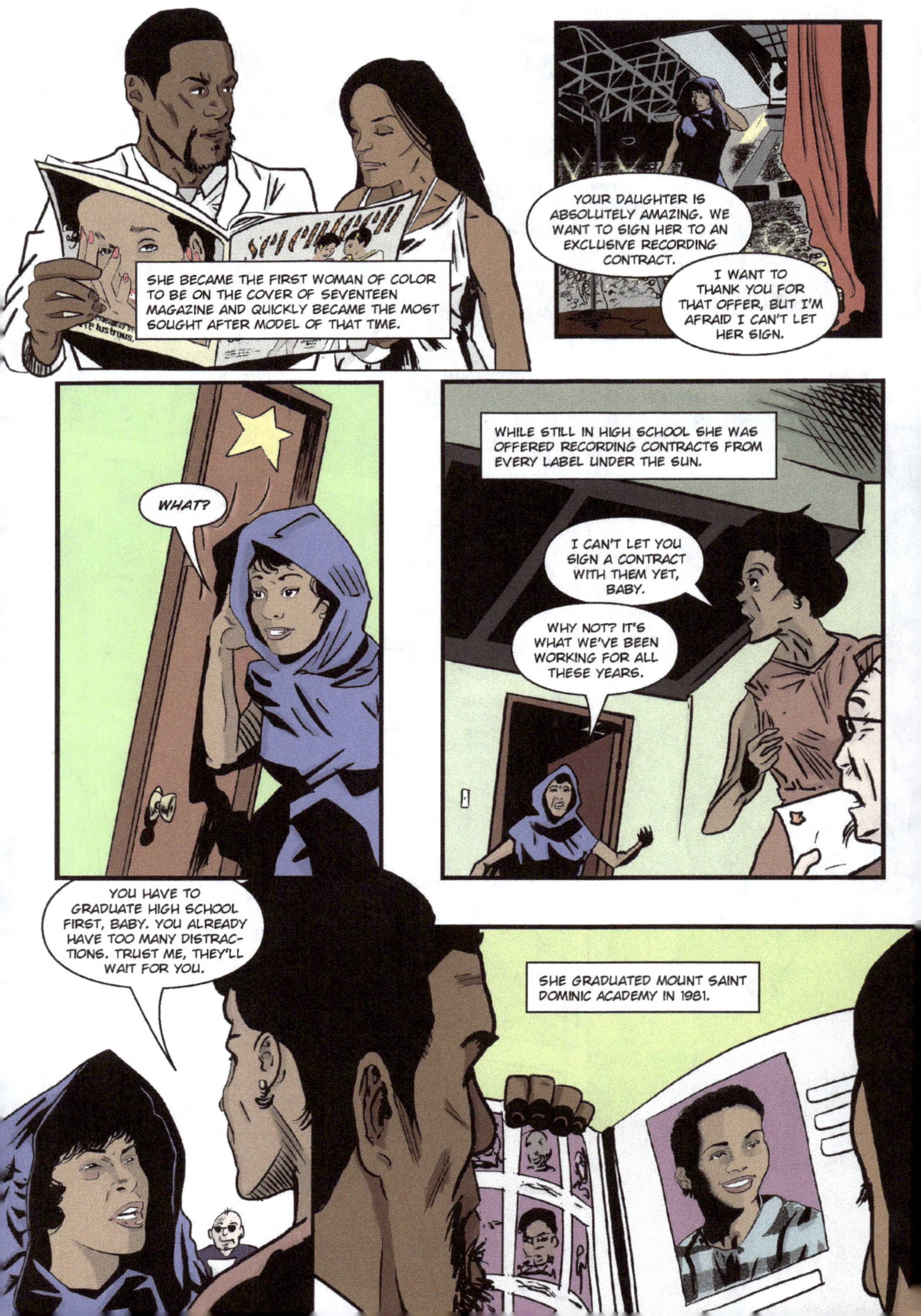

SHE BECAME THE FIRST WOMAN OF COLOR TO BE ON THE COVER OF SEVENTEEN MAGAZINE AND QUICKLY BECAME THE MOST SOUGHT AFTER MODEL OF THAT TIME.
YOUR DAUGHTER IS ABSOLUTELY AMAZING. WE WANT TO SIGN HER TO AN EXCLUSIVE RECORDING CONTRACT.
I WANT TO THANK YOU FOR THAT OFFER, BUT I'M AFRAID I CAN'T LET HER SIGN.
WHAT?
WHILE STILL IN HIGH SCHOOL SHE WAS OFFERED RECORDING CONTRACTS FROM EVERY LABEL UNDER THE SUN.
I CAN'T LET YOU SIGN A CONTRACT WITH THEM YET, BABY.
WHY NOT? IT'S WHAT WE'VE BEEN WORKING FOR ALL THESE YEARS.
YOU HAVE TO GRADUATE HIGH SCHOOL FIRST, BABY. YOU ALREADY HAVE TOO MANY DISTRAC-TIONS. TRUST ME, THEY'LL WAIT FOR YOU.
SHE GRADUATED MOUNT SAINT DOMINIC ACADEMY IN 1981.

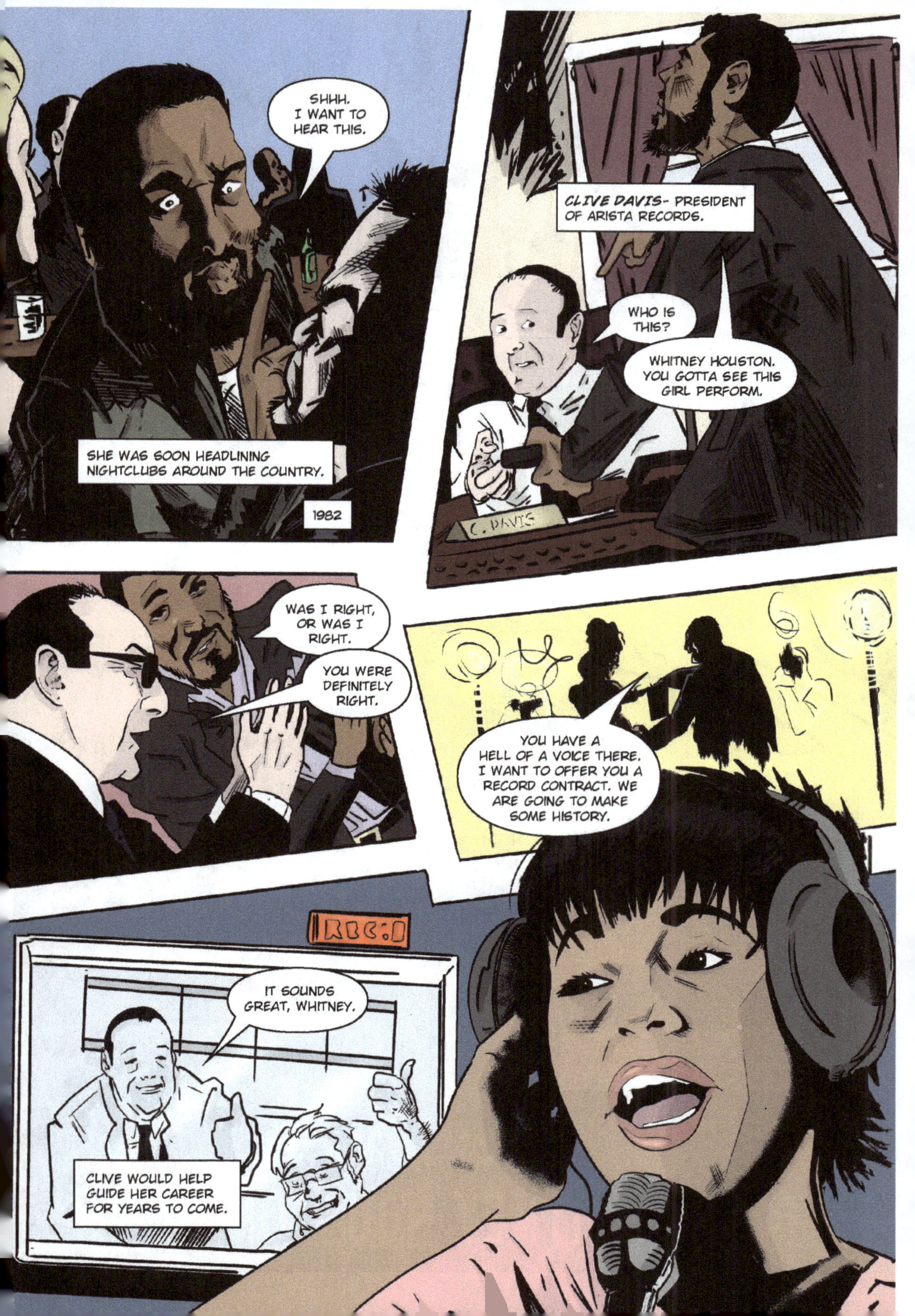
SHHH.
I WANT TO
HEAR THIS.
SHE WAS SOON HEADLINING
NIGHTCLUBS AROUND THE COUNTRY.
1982
CLIVE DAVIS- PRESIDENT
OF ARISTA RECORDS.
WHO IS
THIS?
WHITNEY HOUSTON.
YOU GOTTA SEE THIS
GIRL PERFORM.
C. DAVIS
WAS I RIGHT,
OR WAS I
RIGHT.
YOU WERE
DEFINITELY
RIGHT.
YOU HAVE A
HELL OF A VOICE THERE.
I WANT TO OFFER YOU A
RECORD CONTRACT. WE
ARE GOING TO MAKE
SOME HISTORY.
REC:
IT SOUNDS
GREAT, WHITNEY.
CLIVE WOULD HELP
GUIDE HER CAREER
FOR YEARS TO COME.

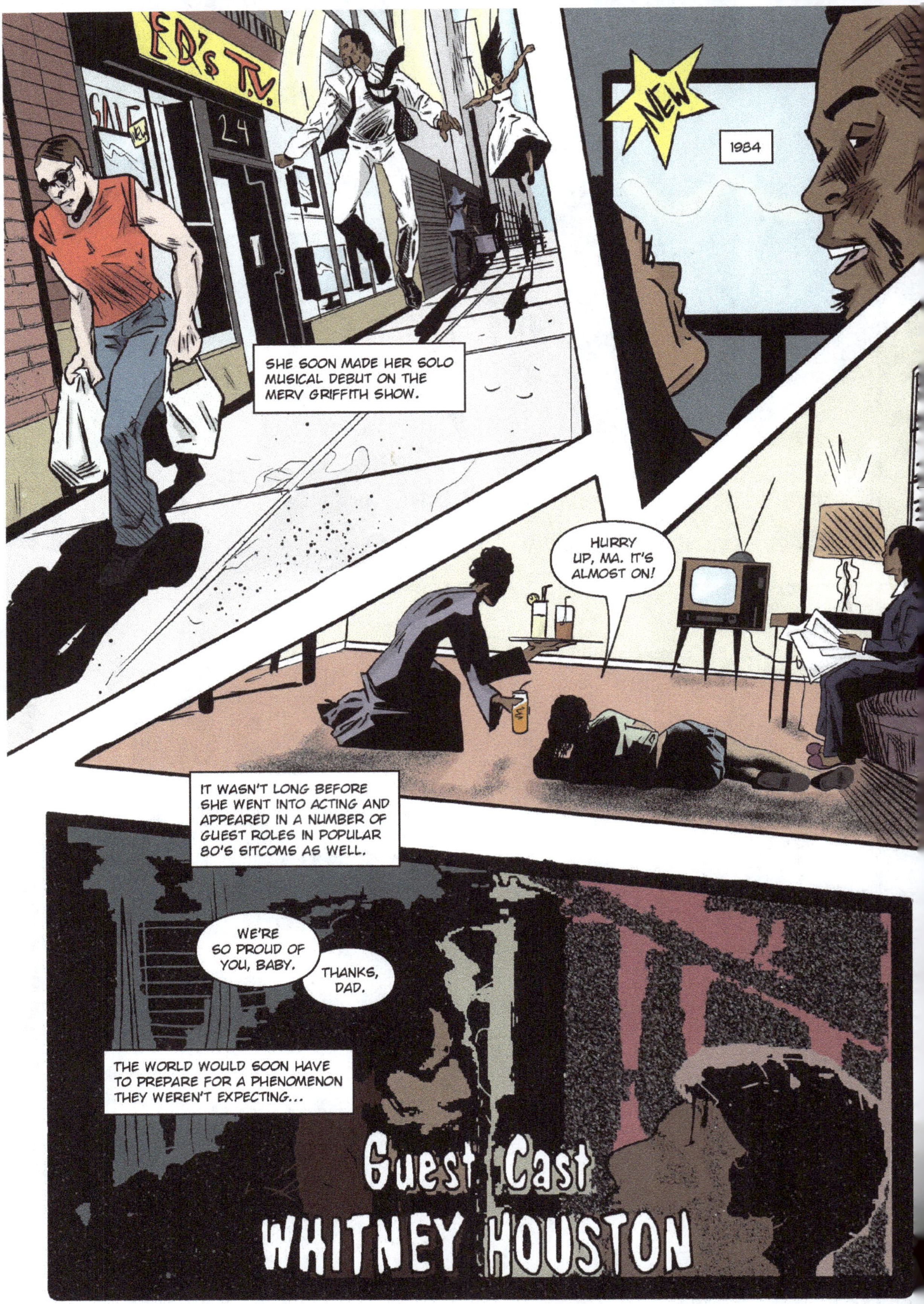
ED's T.V.
SALE
24
SHE SOON MADE HER SOLO MUSICAL DEBUT ON THE MERV GRIFFITH SHOW.
NEW
1984
HURRY UP, MA. IT'S ALMOST ON!
IT WASN'T LONG BEFORE SHE WENT INTO ACTING AND APPEARED IN A NUMBER OF GUEST ROLES IN POPULAR 80'S SITCOMS AS WELL.
WE'RE SO PROUD OF YOU, BABY.
THANKS, DAD.
THE WORLD WOULD SOON HAVE TO PREPARE FOR A PHENOMENON THEY WEREN'T EXPECTING...
Guest Cast
WHITNEY HOUSTON

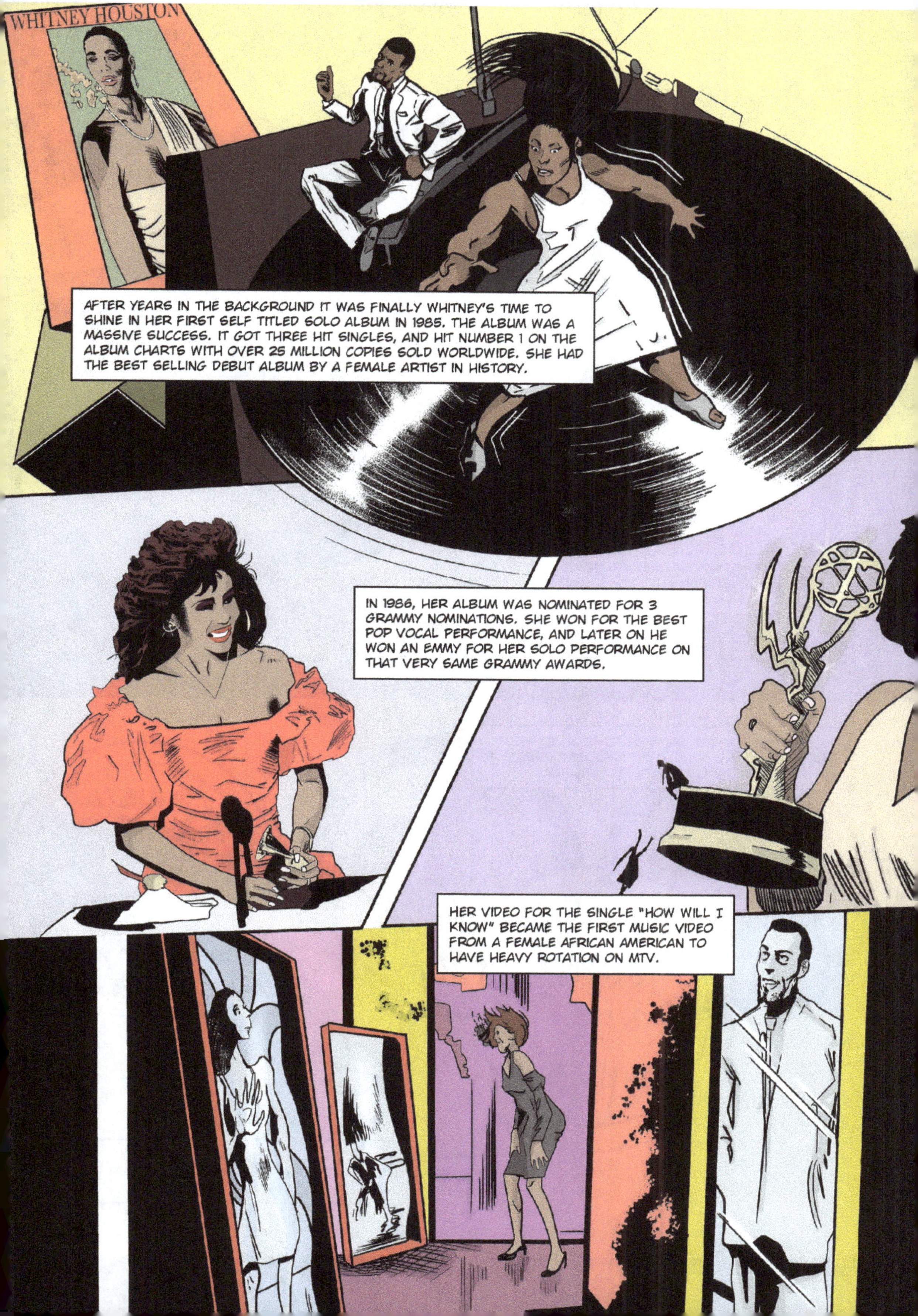
WHITNEY HOUSTON
AFTER YEARS IN THE BACKGROUND IT WAS FINALLY WHITNEY'S TIME TO SHINE IN HER FIRST SELF TITLED SOLO ALBUM IN 1985. THE ALBUM WAS A MASSIVE SUCCESS. IT GOT THREE HIT SINGLES, AND HIT NUMBER 1 ON THE ALBUM CHARTS WITH OVER 25 MILLION COPIES SOLD WORLDWIDE. SHE HAD THE BEST SELLING DEBUT ALBUM BY A FEMALE ARTIST IN HISTORY.
IN 1986, HER ALBUM WAS NOMINATED FOR 3 GRAMMY NOMINATIONS. SHE WON FOR THE BEST POP VOCAL PERFORMANCE, AND LATER ON HE WON AN EMMY FOR HER SOLO PERFORMANCE ON THAT VERY SAME GRAMMY AWARDS.
HER VIDEO FOR THE SINGLE "HOW WILL I KNOW" BECAME THE FIRST MUSIC VIDEO FROM A FEMALE AFRICAN AMERICAN TO HAVE HEAVY ROTATION ON MTV.

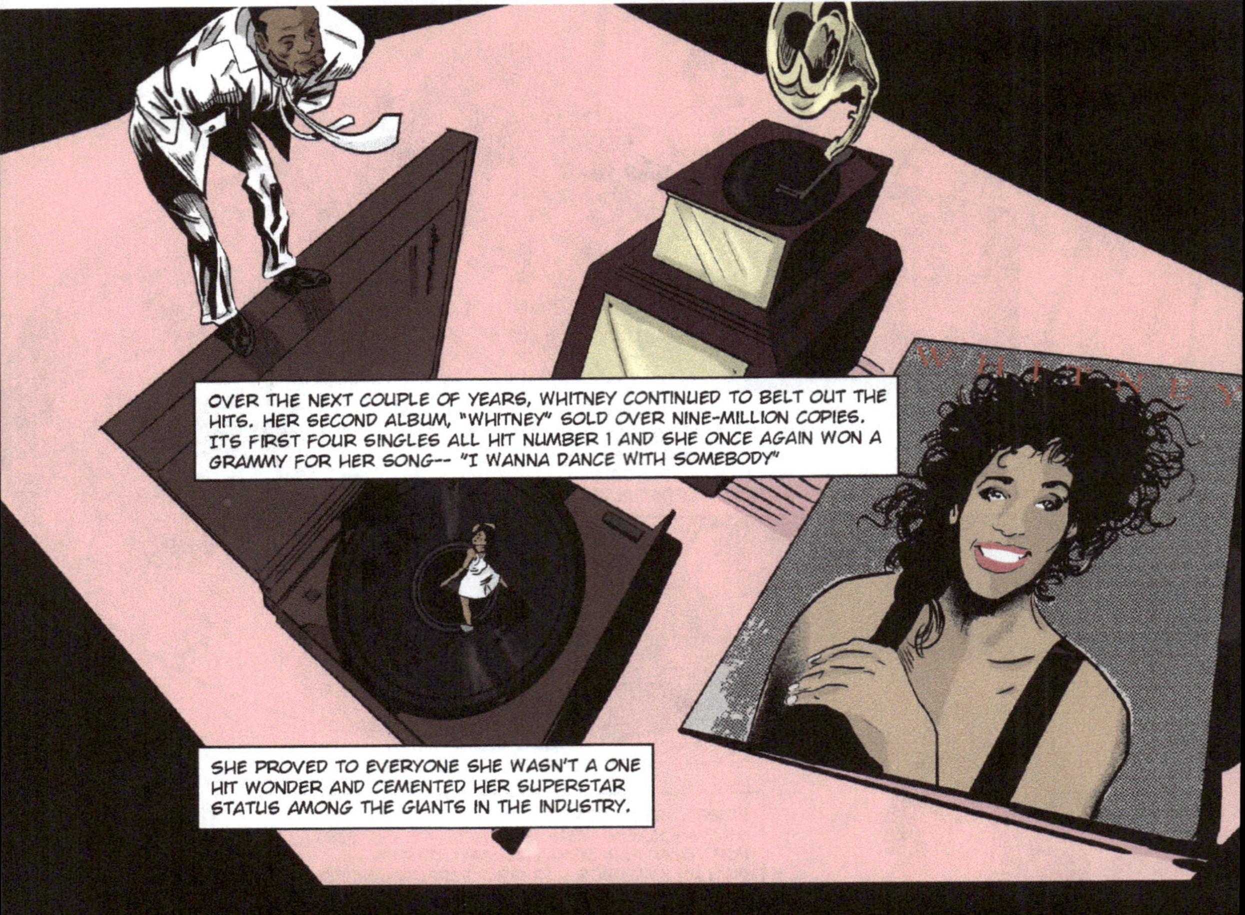
OVER THE NEXT COUPLE OF YEARS, WHITNEY CONTINUED TO BELT OUT THE HITS. HER SECOND ALBUM, "WHITNEY" SOLD OVER NINE-MILLION COPIES. ITS FIRST FOUR SINGLES ALL HIT NUMBER 1 AND SHE ONCE AGAIN WON A GRAMMY FOR HER SONG-- "I WANNA DANCE WITH SOMEBODY"
SHE PROVED TO EVERYONE SHE WASN'T A ONE HIT WONDER AND CEMENTED HER SUPERSTAR STATUS AMONG THE GIANTS IN THE INDUSTRY.

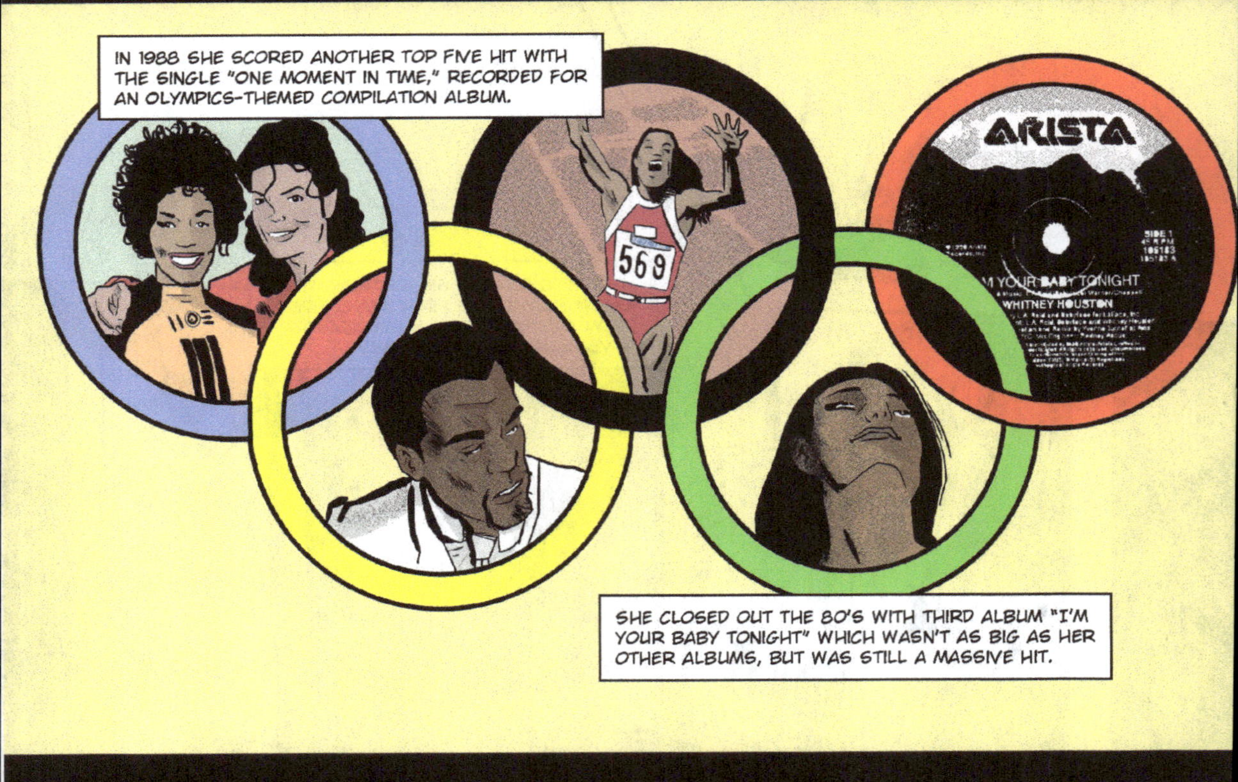
IN 1988 SHE SCORED ANOTHER TOP FIVE HIT WITH THE SINGLE "ONE MOMENT IN TIME," RECORDED FOR AN OLYMPICS-THEMED COMPILATION ALBUM.
569
ARISTA
WHITNEY HOUSTON
SHE CLOSED OUT THE 80'S WITH THIRD ALBUM "I'M YOUR BABY TONIGHT" WHICH WASN'T AS BIG AS HER OTHER ALBUMS, BUT WAS STILL A MASSIVE HIT.

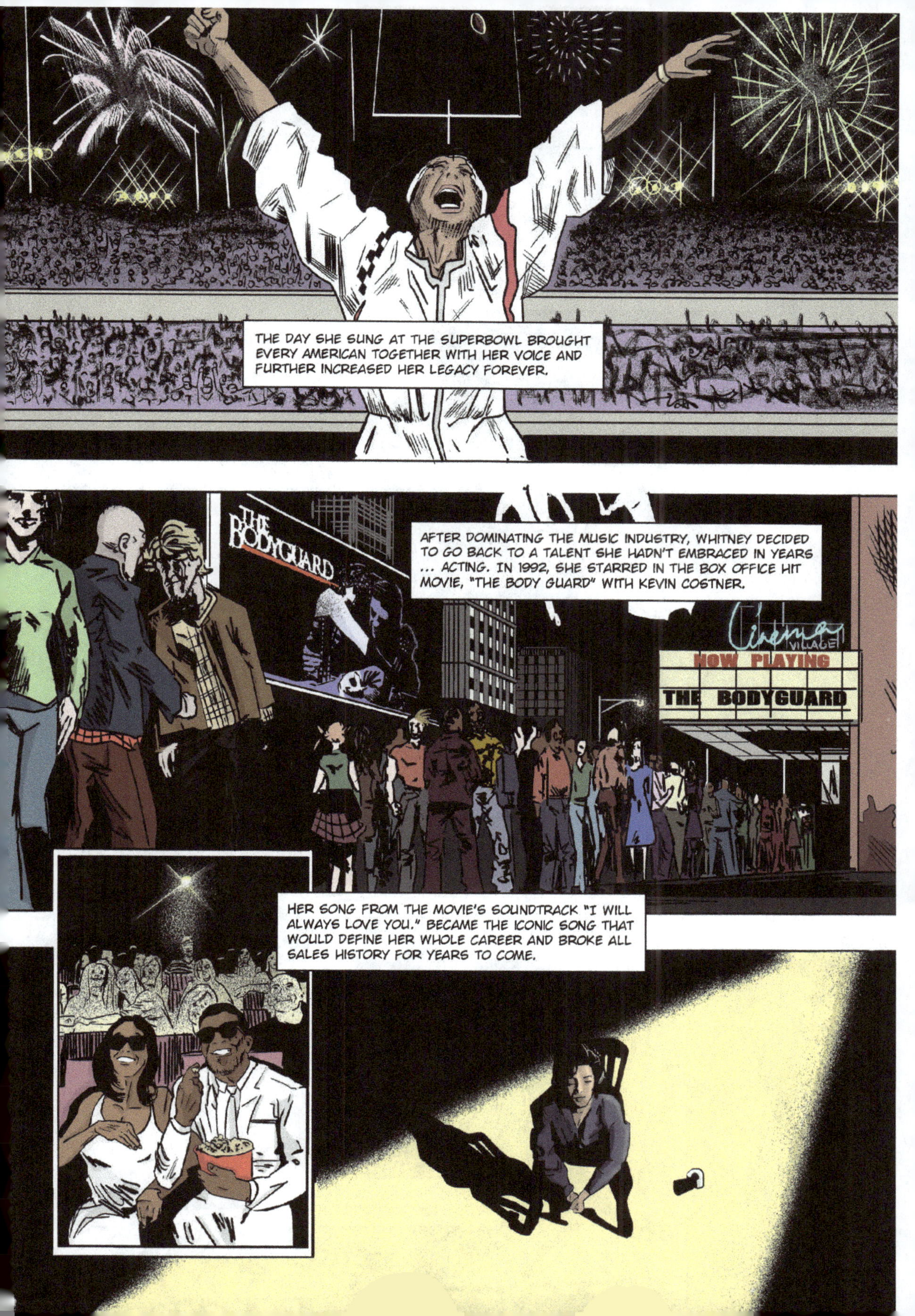
THE DAY SHE SUNG AT THE SUPERBOWL BROUGHT EVERY AMERICAN TOGETHER WITH HER VOICE AND FURTHER INCREASED HER LEGACY FOREVER.
THE BODYGUARD
AFTER DOMINATING THE MUSIC INDUSTRY, WHITNEY DECIDED TO GO BACK TO A TALENT SHE HADN'T EMBRACED IN YEARS ... ACTING. IN 1992, SHE STARRED IN THE BOX OFFICE HIT MOVIE, "THE BODY GUARD" WITH KEVIN COSTNER.
Cinema VILLAGE
NOW PLAYING
THE BODYGUARD
HER SONG FROM THE MOVIE'S SOUNDTRACK "I WILL ALWAYS LOVE YOU." BECAME THE ICONIC SONG THAT WOULD DEFINE HER WHOLE CAREER AND BROKE ALL SALES HISTORY FOR YEARS TO COME.

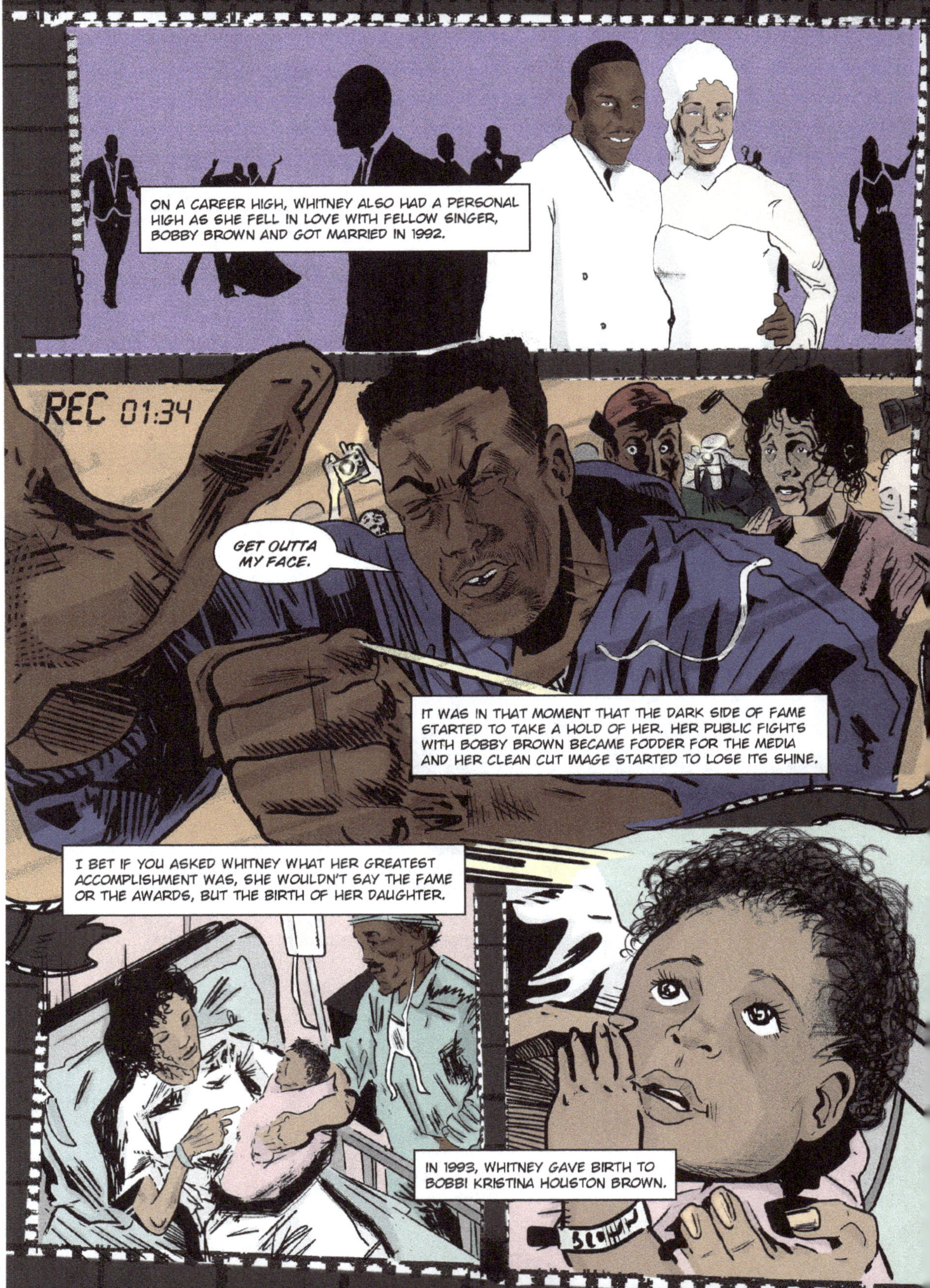

ON A CAREER HIGH, WHITNEY ALSO HAD A PERSONAL HIGH AS SHE FELL IN LOVE WITH FELLOW SINGER, BOBBY BROWN AND GOT MARRIED IN 1992.
REC 01:34
GET OUTTA MY FACE.
IT WAS IN THAT MOMENT THAT THE DARK SIDE OF FAME STARTED TO TAKE A HOLD OF HER. HER PUBLIC FIGHTS WITH BOBBY BROWN BECAME FODDER FOR THE MEDIA AND HER CLEAN CUT IMAGE STARTED TO LOSE ITS SHINE.
I BET IF YOU ASKED WHITNEY WHAT HER GREATEST ACCOMPLISHMENT WAS, SHE WOULDN'T SAY THE FAME OR THE AWARDS, BUT THE BIRTH OF HER DAUGHTER.
IN 1993, WHITNEY GAVE BIRTH TO BOBBI KRISTINA HOUSTON BROWN.

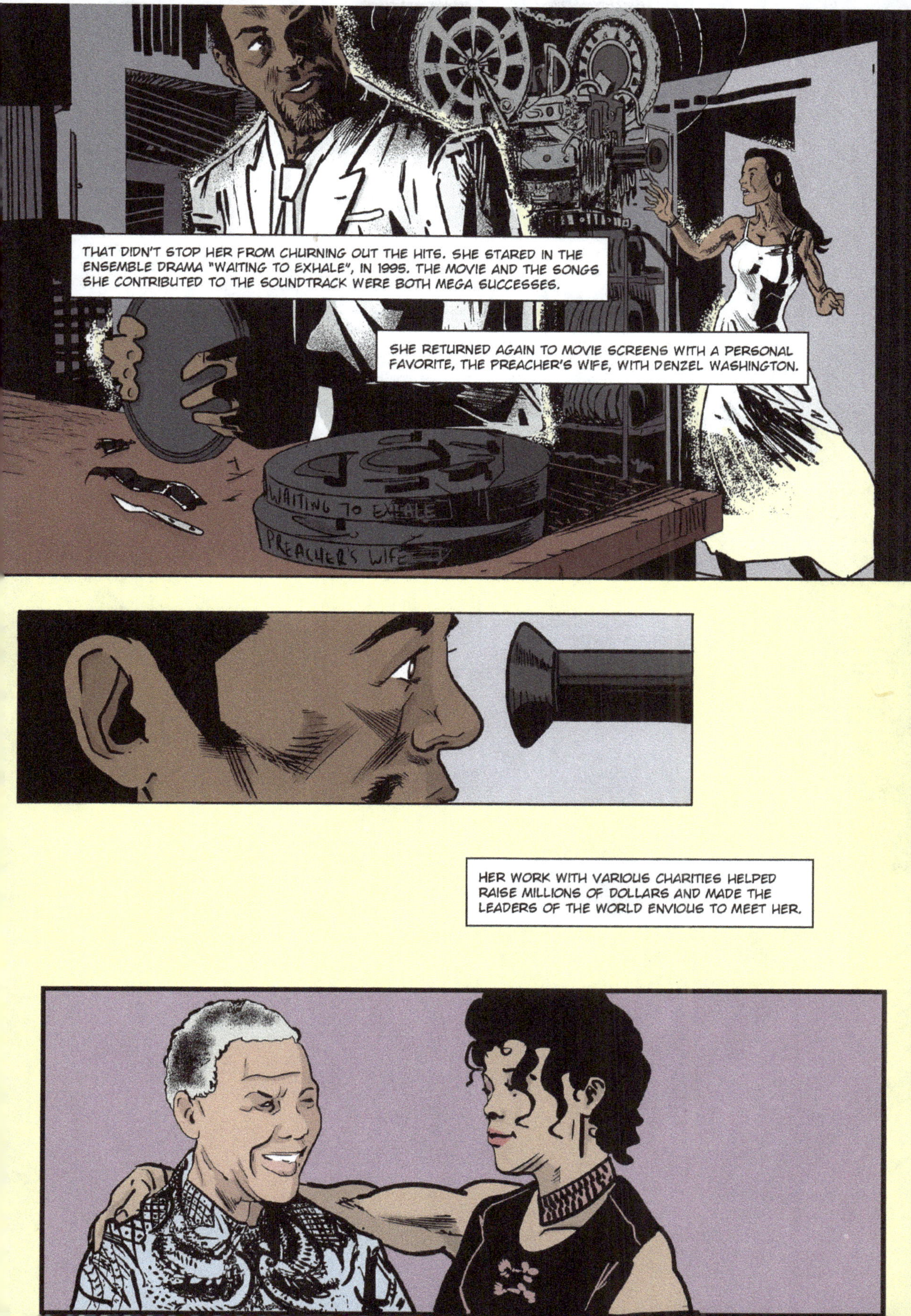
THAT DIDN'T STOP HER FROM CHURNING OUT THE HITS. SHE STARED IN THE ENSEMBLE DRAMA "WAITING TO EXHALE", IN 1995. THE MOVIE AND THE SONGS SHE CONTRIBUTED TO THE SOUNDTRACK WERE BOTH MEGA SUCCESSES.
SHE RETURNED AGAIN TO MOVIE SCREENS WITH A PERSONAL FAVORITE, THE PREACHER'S WIFE, WITH DENZEL WASHINGTON.
WAITING TO EXHALE
PREACHER'S WIFE
HER WORK WITH VARIOUS CHARITIES HELPED RAISE MILLIONS OF DOLLARS AND MADE THE LEADERS OF THE WORLD ENVIOUS TO MEET HER.

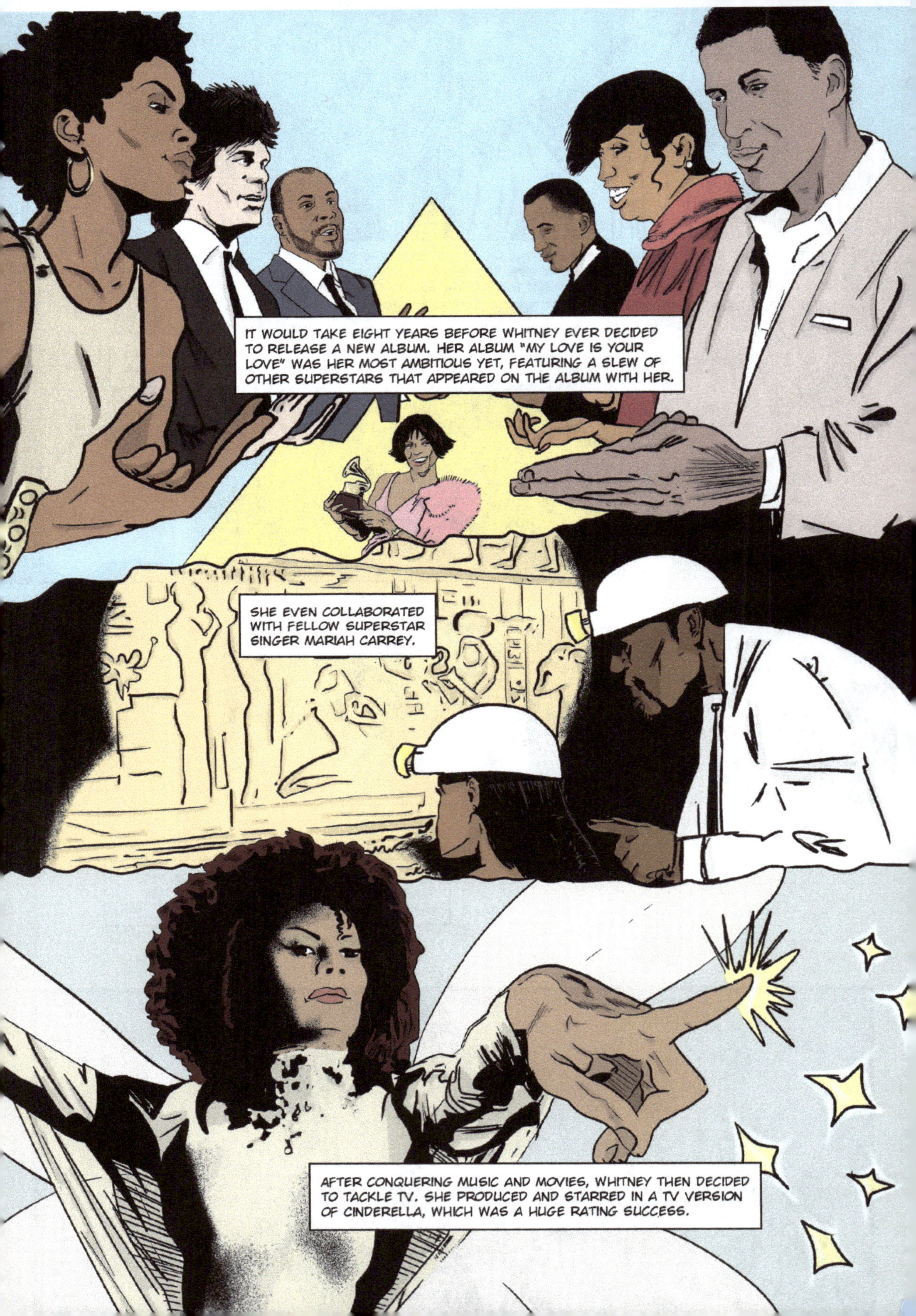
IT WOULD TAKE EIGHT YEARS BEFORE WHITNEY EVER DECIDED TO RELEASE A NEW ALBUM. HER ALBUM "MY LOVE IS YOUR LOVE" WAS HER MOST AMBITIOUS YET, FEATURING A SLEW OF OTHER SUPERSTARS THAT APPEARED ON THE ALBUM WITH HER.
SHE EVEN COLLABORATED WITH FELLOW SUPERSTAR SINGER MARIAH CARREY.
AFTER CONQUERING MUSIC AND MOVIES, WHITNEY THEN DECIDED TO TACKLE TV. SHE PRODUCED AND STARRED IN A TV VERSION OF CINDERELLA, WHICH WAS A HUGE RATING SUCCESS.

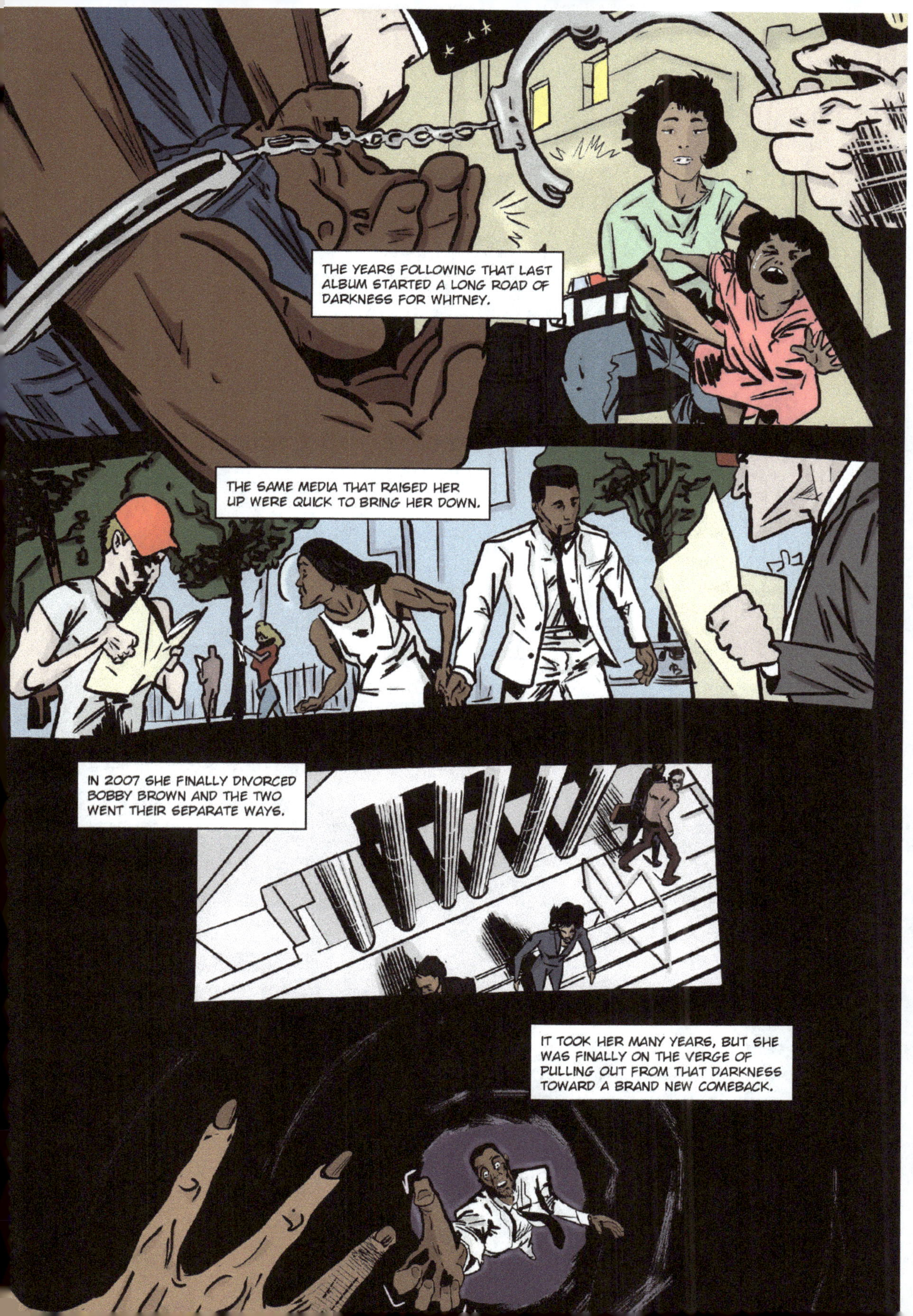
THE YEARS FOLLOWING THAT LAST ALBUM STARTED A LONG ROAD OF DARKNESS FOR WHITNEY.
THE SAME MEDIA THAT RAISED HER UP WERE QUICK TO BRING HER DOWN.
IN 2007 SHE FINALLY DIVORCED BOBBY BROWN AND THE TWO WENT THEIR SEPARATE WAYS.
IT TOOK HER MANY YEARS, BUT SHE WAS FINALLY ON THE VERGE OF PULLING OUT FROM THAT DARKNESS TOWARD A BRAND NEW COMEBACK.

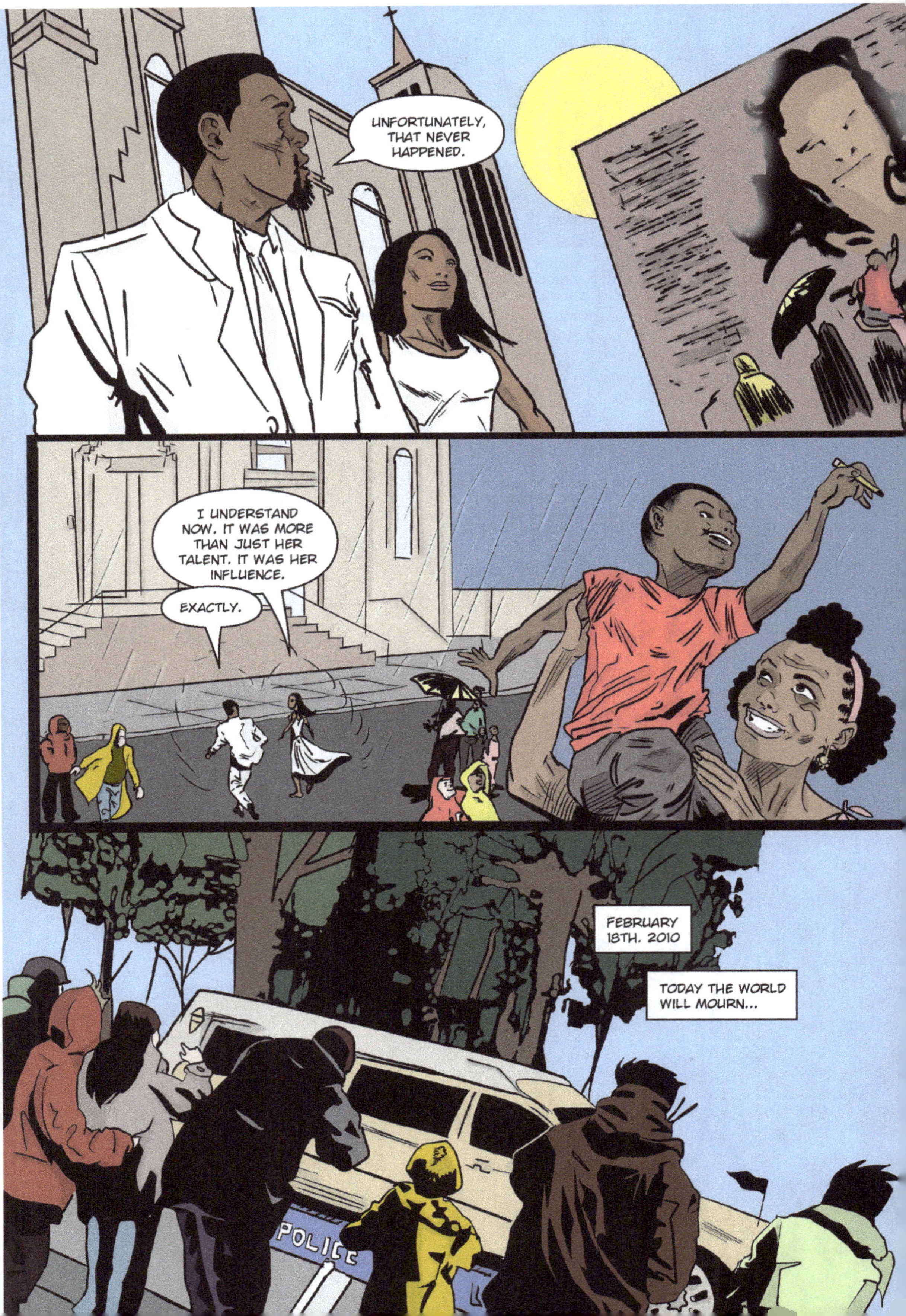
UNFORTUNATELY, THAT NEVER HAPPENED.
I UNDERSTAND NOW. IT WAS MORE THAN JUST HER TALENT. IT WAS HER INFLUENCE.
EXACTLY.
FEBRUARY 18TH. 2010
TODAY THE WORLD WILL MOURN...
POLICE

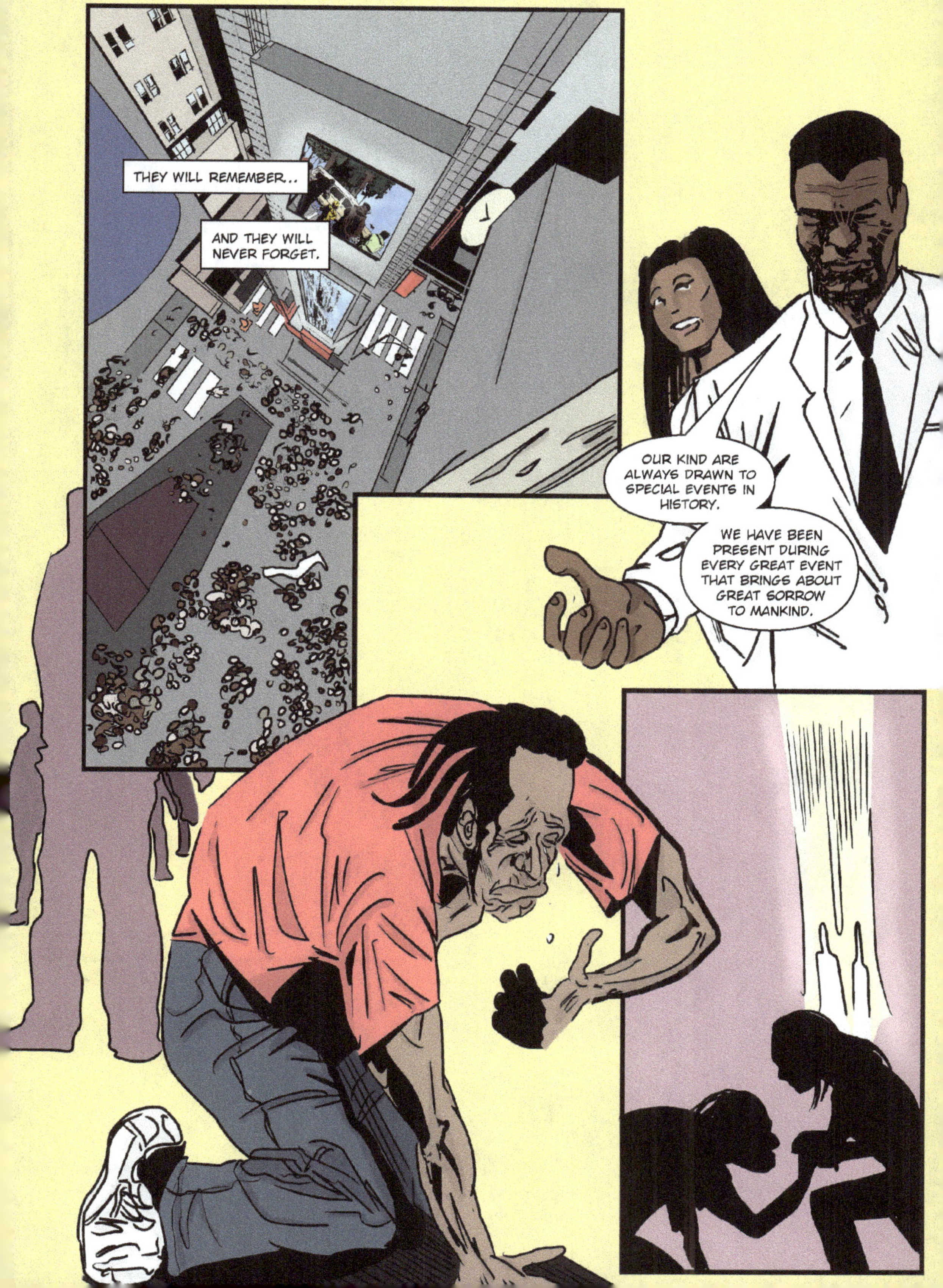
THEY WILL REMEMBER..
AND THEY WILL NEVER FORGET.
OUR KIND ARE ALWAYS DRAWN TO SPECIAL EVENTS IN HISTORY.
WE HAVE BEEN PRESENT DURING EVERY GREAT EVENT THAT BRINGS ABOUT GREAT SORROW TO MANKIND.

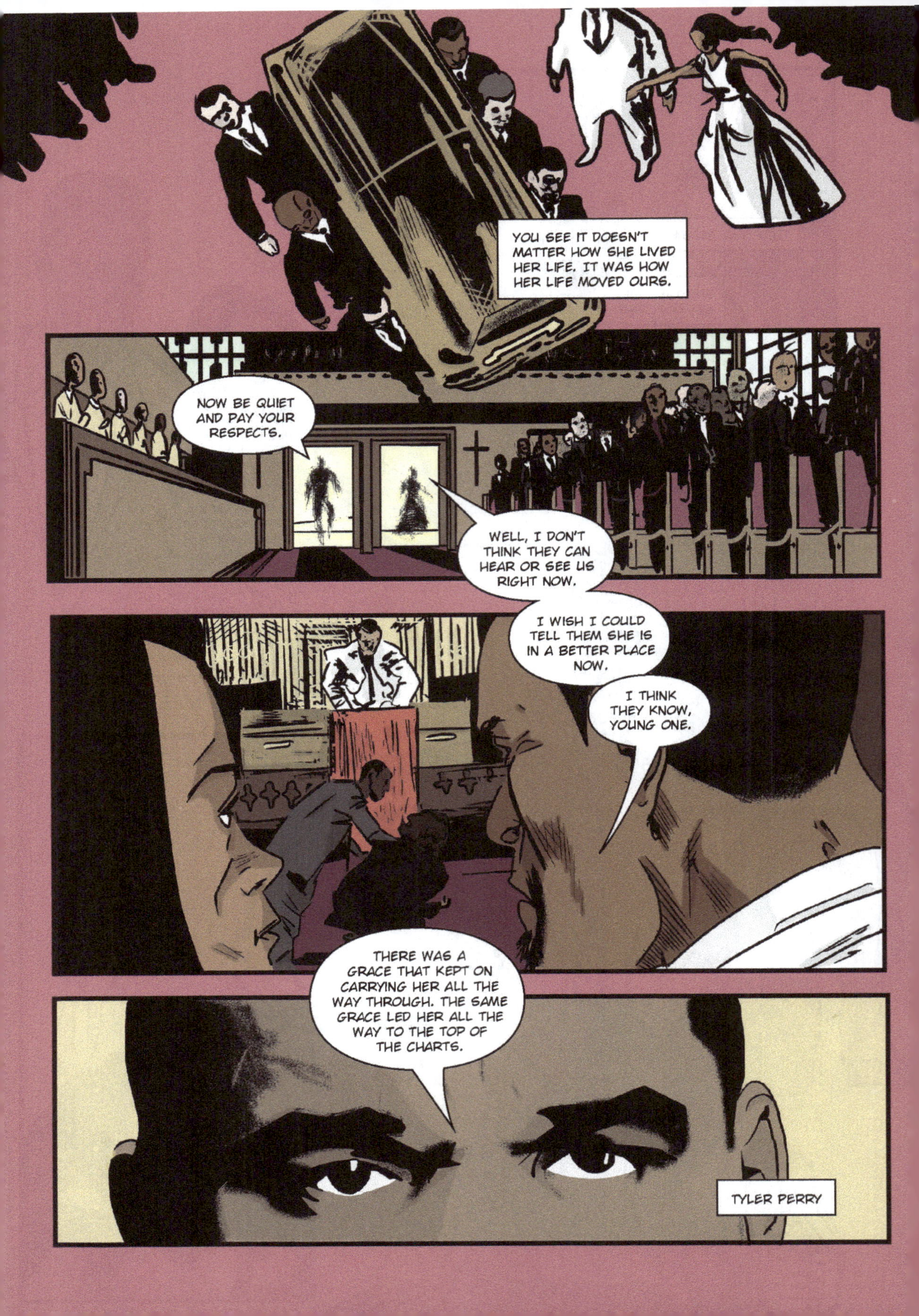
YOU SEE IT DOESN'T MATTER HOW SHE LIVED HER LIFE. IT WAS HOW HER LIFE MOVED OURS.
NOW BE QUIET AND PAY YOUR RESPECTS.
WELL, I DON'T THINK THEY CAN HEAR OR SEE US RIGHT NOW.
I WISH I COULD TELL THEM SHE IS IN A BETTER PLACE NOW.
I THINK THEY KNOW, YOUNG ONE.
THERE WAS A GRACE THAT KEPT ON CARRYING HER ALL THE WAY THROUGH. THE SAME GRACE LED HER ALL THE WAY TO THE TOP OF THE CHARTS.
TYLER PERRY

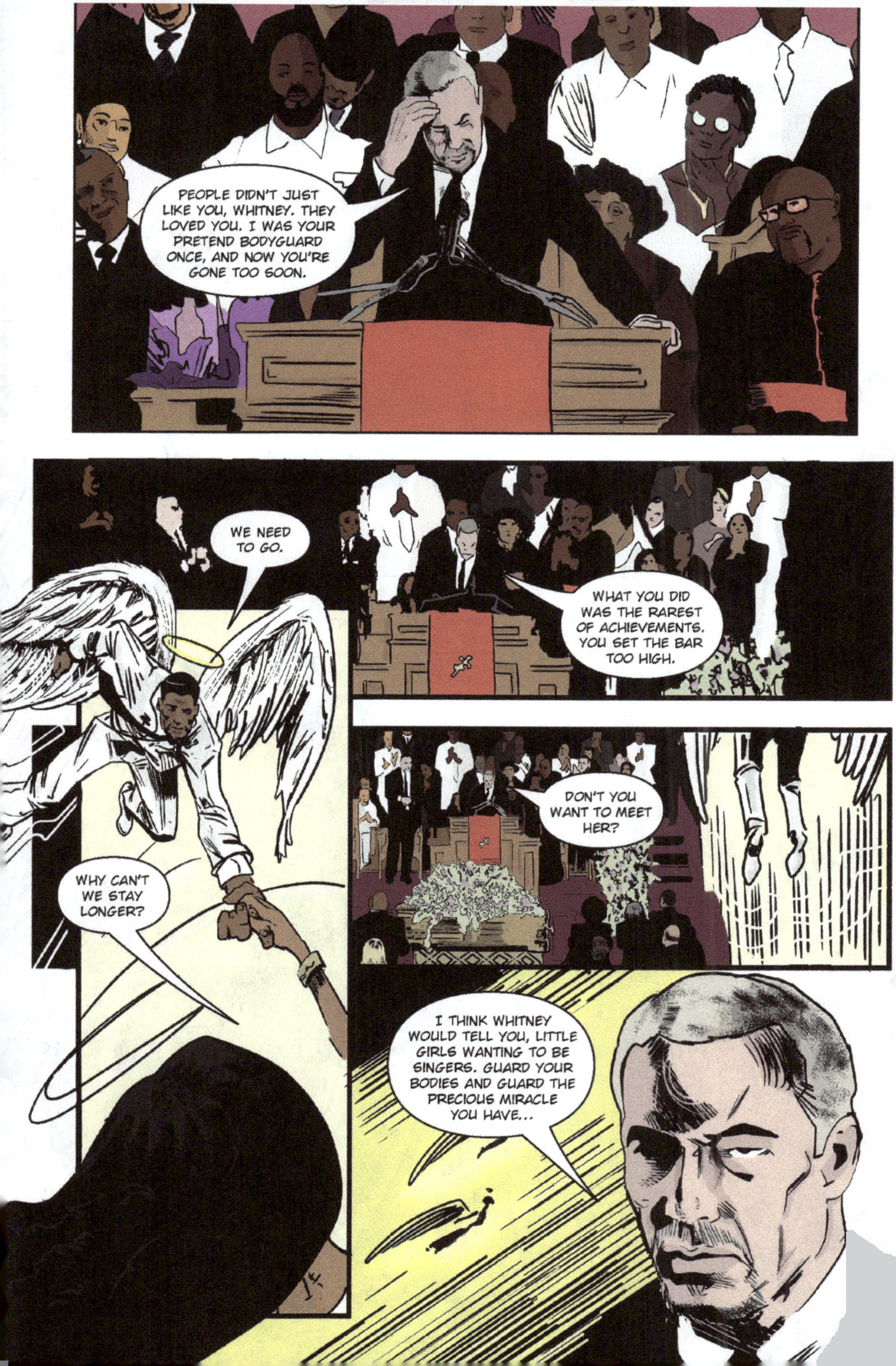
PEOPLE DIDN'T JUST LIKE YOU, WHITNEY. THEY LOVED YOU. I WAS YOUR PRETEND BODYGUARD ONCE, AND NOW YOU'RE GONE TOO SOON.
WE NEED TO GO.
WHAT YOU DID WAS THE RAREST OF ACHIEVEMENTS. YOU SET THE BAR TOO HIGH.
WHY CAN'T WE STAY LONGER?
DON'T YOU WANT TO MEET HER?
I THINK WHITNEY WOULD TELL YOU, LITTLE GIRLS WANTING TO BE SINGERS. GUARD YOUR BODIES AND GUARD THE PRECIOUS MIRACLE YOU HAVE...

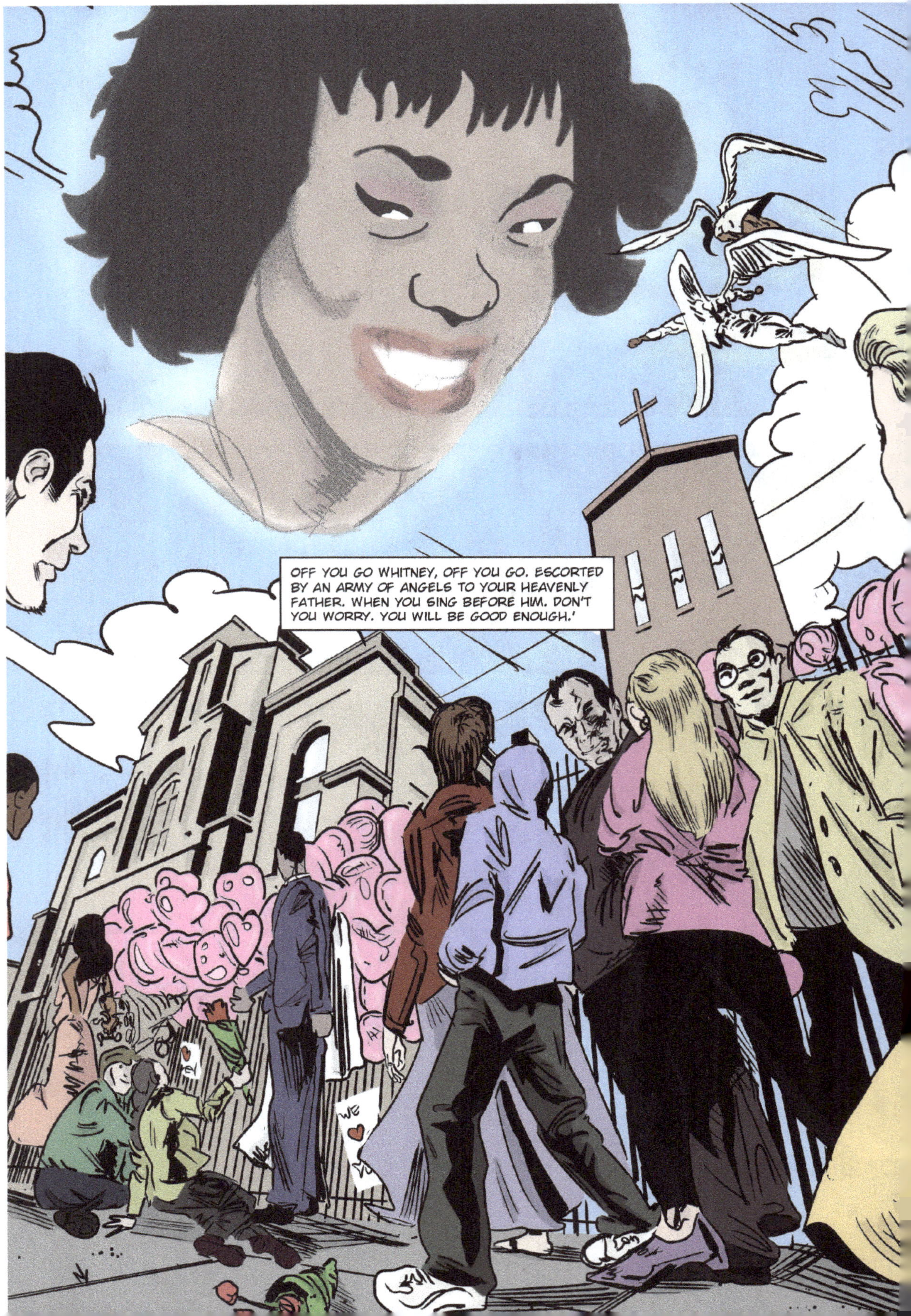
OFF YOU GO WHITNEY, OFF YOU GO. ESCORTED BY AN ARMY OF ANGELS TO YOUR HEAVENLY FATHER. WHEN YOU SING BEFORE HIM. DON'T YOU WORRY. YOU WILL BE GOOD ENOUGH.'

BLUEWATER COMICS

Raphael Moran —————————————————— **Writer**

Kirk Feretzanis —————————————————— **Penciler**

Dan Barnes —————————————————— **Colorist**

David Hopkins —————————————————— **Letterer**

Neil Feigeles —————————————————— **Cover**

Darren G. Davis
Publisher

Jason Schultz
Vice President

Jarred Weisfeld
Literary Manager

Kailey Marsh
Entertainment Manager

Maggie Jessup
Publicity

BLUEWATER COMICS

www.bluewaterprod.com

#ERASEHATE WITH THE MATTHEW SHEPARD FOUNDATION

With your donated dollars and volunteer hours, we work tirelessly to erase hate from every corner of America through our programs.

SPEAKING ENGAGEMENTS

Since Matt's death in 1998, Judy and Dennis have been determined to prevent others from similar tragedies. By sharing their story, they are able to carry on Matt's legacy.

HATE CRIMES REPORTING

Our work to improve reporting includes conducting trainings for law enforcement agencies, building relationships between community leaders and law enforcement, and developing policy reform in reporting practices.

LARAMIE PROJECT

MSF offers support to productions of The Laramie Project, which depicts the events leading up to and after Matt's murder. It remains one of the most performed plays in America.

MATTHEW'S PLACE

MatthewsPlace.com is a blog designed to provide young LGBTQ+ people with an outlet for their voices. From finance to health to love and dating, and everything in between, our writers contribute excellent material.

Erase Hate

Matthew Shepard Foundation
embracing diversity

www.ingramcontent.com/pod-product-compliance
Lightning Source LLC
Chambersburg PA
CBHW081236020426
42331CB00012B/3200